THE PRADO

Treasures of
THE PRADO

Felipe Vicente Garín Llombart

A TINY FOLIO™
Abbeville Press Publishers
New York London Paris

For copyright and Cataloging-in-Publication Data, see page 312.

CONTENTS

INTRODUCTION

When it opened on November 19, 1819, the Royal Museum of Painting and Sculpture of the Prado consisted entirely of works from the royal collections, previously on view in the palaces of the Spanish sovereigns. The uniqueness of the Prado's collection today is largely attributable to this original core of works, which reflect the artistic tastes of Spain's monarchs. Their choices resulted in the Prado's exceptional collection of paintings by Diego Velázquez and Francisco de Goya (both of whom served as court painters), and in the multitude of fine works by Titian, Peter Paul Rubens, and Hieronymus Bosch. At the same time, their choices inevitably led to some of the collection's lacunae.

In order to appreciate the tremendous strength of the Prado's holdings, we must first understand the history of royal collecting in Spain, which had begun centuries before the museum opened. Isabella the Catholic acquired a rich collection of Flemish paintings, which she bequeathed to the royal chapel of the Cathedral of Granada in 1504. Under Emperor Charles V (1516–56) and especially Philip II (1556–98), Flemish and Italian painting became the cornerstone of the royal collections. Titian met Charles V in 1532, and he painted for him and for Philip II a variety of portraits, mythological scenes, and devotional works; his *Danaë and the Shower of Gold* and *The Emperor Charles V at Mühlberg* were central elements in the decor of the royal palaces. Philip II was also partial to Flemish altarpieces like Rogier van der Weyden's *Descent from the Cross,* and his eclectic taste led him to purchase several paintings by Bosch, which rank among the treasures of the Prado. The role of the court painters, in particular that of portraitists like Antonio Moro and Alonso Sánchez Coello, also expanded considerably under Philip II's reign.

Philip IV (1621–65), Velázquez's patron for over thirty years and one of the greatest collectors of the seventeenth century, acquired nearly two thousand French and Italian paintings by both Renaissance and contemporary artists. When the possessions of England's Charles I were dispersed after his execution, Philip IV strengthened his Italian Renaissance holdings even more by acquiring new works by Correggio, Andrea del Sarto, and Titian, as well as Andrea Mantegna's *Death of the Virgin* and Raphael's *Holy Family with a Lamb.* To ornament his palaces he turned to landscapists from Rome as well as to Rubens, and his predilection for Rubens— whom he knew personally and from whom he commissioned a set of works after Ovid's *Metamorphoses* for his hunting pavilion—led him to purchase several paintings still in Rubens's studio at the time of the painter's death. Philip IV also decided to donate his collection to the crown, thereby eliminating the risk of future dispersion and even laying the conceptual foundation for the future Prado.

A fire at the royal palace in Madrid in 1734 and the resulting loss of more than five hundred works cast a shadow over the reign of Philip V (1724–46), grandson of the French king Louis XIV and the first Bourbon king of Spain. Nevertheless, Philip's French heritage and the role played by his second wife, Isabella Farnese, breathed fresh life into the collections and into the new buildings commissioned to replace the royal palace. Isabella Farnese, who astutely acquired important works by Bartolomé Esteban Murillo, also reinforced the traditional Spanish taste for Italian painting, and Italian fresco painters from Corrado Giaquinto to Giambattista Tiepolo were summoned to decorate the new palaces. (Many of their sketches remain in the Prado's collection.)

This vast decorative enterprise, which was continued by Ferdinand VI (1746–59) and Charles III (1759–88), also yielded commissions for the Santa Barbara tapestry workshops. An entire generation of young Spaniards trained at the new Academy of Fine Arts was called on to design cartoons for tapestries, and those by Goya are among the Prado's treasures. In addition, his portraits of

Charles IV (1788–1808) and the royal family constitute a grand finale for the royal collections in the years just before they were opened to the public.

The idea of exhibiting the collections was first broached in 1775 by Anton Raphael Mengs, a painter, theorist, and guiding spirit of the Academy; that same year plans for a museum building were submitted by the great Neoclassical architect Juan de Villanueva. Construction of the building, which was intended to house both works of art and works of science (Villanueva also designed the Astronomical Observatory and the Botanical Gardens), continued desultorily over several decades, interrupted first by the death of Charles III toward the end of 1788 and then by the Napoleonic wars.

In 1809 Joseph Bonaparte, king of Spain from 1808 to 1814 during the Napoleonic usurpation, decided to establish a museum of paintings comprising works from the royal collections and those confiscated from the religious orders, which had recently been suppressed. This museum, which came to be known as the Museo Josefino, was to have been installed in the Buenavista Palace, but its progress was halted by the fall of the Napoleonic empire. There is a certain irony in the fact that the first attempt at opening a national museum was given impetus by a Napoleonic king and that it coincided with the Napoleonic wars, which led to the disappearance of so many important works from Spanish soil.

After the fall of Joseph Bonaparte and the restoration of the Bourbons, Ferdinand VII (1814–33) renewed the museum project, but the convents' demands for the return of their paintings curtailed his plans considerably. With the support of his queen, Isabella of Braganza, he decided to place works from the royal collections on public display, and charged his majordomo, the Marquis of Santa Cruz, with the task of organizing this gallery; Santa Cruz in turn was aided by Vicente Lopez, First Painter to the Chamber. On March 3, 1818, the king ordered the restoration of Villanueva's superb Neoclassical building, begun in 1775, which had become the Museum of Natural History. Its construction had been well advanced by the time of Joseph Bonaparte's rule, but it had been heavily damaged during the wars and at one point had even been used to house French troops.

Ferdinand VII, who underwrote the repairs with his own personal funds, wanted the museum to be the setting for "the most beautiful paintings decorating his palaces." So it became. When it opened in November 1819 the museum already boasted more than fifteen hundred works, but the unusually uncrowded style of installation and the lack of display space meant that only a small portion of them could be shown. All were catalogued gradually, one room at a time, by the curator, Luis Eusebi.

Though still owned by the crown and thus part of the king's estate at his death in 1833, the works in the Prado were not divided between his two daughters—a decision crucial to the museum's future. They went instead to Isabella II (1833–68), who compensated her sister for them. Throughout these years the Prado was continually enriched by the addition of works from the royal palaces, especially the Escorial, and of those purchased by successive rulers. In 1839 the Dauphin's Treasure entered the museum; a little later came drawings from the studios of the court painters. The Prado's collection of drawings now contains almost five thousand works, including those from the court painters and from the substantial bequest made by Pedro Fernández Durán in 1930. Most are Spanish and Italian.

In 1843 the first catalog of the collection, by Pedro de Madrazo, was published, incorporating 1,833 entries; the 1858 edition contained 2,001. The fall and exile of Isabella II in 1868 led to the dissolution of royal property rights and the reversion of all royal goods to the state. At that point the royal collection, still the core of today's Prado Museum, consisted of more than three thousand paintings.

In 1870 another collection entered the Prado, that of the National Museum of Painting and Sculpture (commonly known as the Trinity Museum, after the Convent of the Trinity in Madrid, where it was housed).

The museum had been founded in 1836 to display works that had been seized from convents and monasteries in Madrid, Toledo, Avila, and Segovia under the Disentailment Decree, which had suppressed the religious orders and demanded the confiscation of church goods. There were 1,733 items in all, most of them from the seventeenth century.

The third core of the museum's collection consists of acquisitions made since 1856 through purchases, bequests, gifts, offerings in lieu of taxes, and so on. In 1915 Pablo Bosch donated eighty-nine paintings, including several precious works by the Spanish Primitives (from the Gothic period); the Fernández Durán bequest of 1930 encompassed more than three thousand drawings, paintings, and objets d'art. Seeking to fill a serious gap in the collections, Francisco Cambó gave the Prado several Italian Renaissance treasures, including Sandro Botticelli's *Story of Nastagio degli Onesti.* Recently, funds from the Villaescusa Ferrero estate have made possible the purchase of two works by famous painters previously unrepresented in the museum: the *Hurdy-Gurdy Player with a Ribbon,* by Georges de La Tour, and a still life by Juan Sánchez Cotán. These are only a few of the many donations.

From 1856 on, prize-winning works from the National Fine Arts Exhibitions constituted a significant proportion of the Prado's acquisitions. They were often placed in government offices or newly established provincial museums, as were many other canvases from the Prado. That lending practice, which was poorly implemented, ended a few years ago and has led to a reevaluation of the collections.

The entire collection of works from the National Fine Arts Exhibitions left the Prado in 1894, upon creation of the Museum of Modern Art; they returned in 1971, after the Casón del Buen Retiro was designated to house works by nineteenth-century Spanish masters. The Casón del Buen Retiro, located just a five-minute walk from the Prado, was formerly the ballroom of the Buen Retiro Palace, used for the entertainment of Philip IV and his court. This, along with the wing containing the Hall of Realms (now the Army Museum), is all that remains of the original structure, which was seriously damaged during the Napoleonic wars. It was transformed in the nineteenth century to house the Senate and features a splendid ceiling fresco representing *The Order of the Golden Fleece,* painted by Luca Giordano during his Spanish sojourn at the end of the seventeenth century. From 1981 to 1992 Picasso's celebrated *Guernica,* painted for the Spanish Pavilion of the 1937 Paris World's Fair, was displayed here. Today this work hangs in the Centro de Arte Reina Sofía, the newly established national museum of contemporary art in Madrid.

The Prado suffered through perilous and heroic times during the Spanish Civil War (1936–39). Because the museum had attained considerable symbolic and political significance, its most important works (361 paintings, 184 drawings, and the Dauphin's Treasure) were removed shortly after the first bombs fell on Madrid in November 1936. They followed the republican government in its peregrinations—first to Valencia, then to Catalonia, Perlada, and Figueras.

When the fall of Catalonia was imminent, in February 1939, an agreement was reached between the republican government and an international committee led by the painter José Maria Sert. The Prado's art works, along with others from various Spanish institutions, were transported by truck across the Pyrenees, then given a temporary home in Geneva, in the Palace of the League of Nations. Some of these treasures were exhibited at the Museum of Art and History in Geneva during the summer of 1939, after peace was restored in Spain; the display of so many masterpieces riveted all who saw them. The exhibition closed on August 31, and the works were traveling through France on September 3, just as World War II exploded.

Over the last twelve years the Prado has been conducting an important campaign of renovation, which includes the installation of air conditioning and improved lighting. The implementation of expansion plans—restoring the Army Museum and the Formento Palace, as well as the Botanical Gardens—will well serve the interests of the Prado's two million annual visitors by placing more of the museum's sublime collection on display.

SPANISH PAINTING, SCULPTURE, AND DRAWING

The Prado's unparalleled wealth of Spanish paintings includes works of every era, from the Romanesque to the nineteenth century, both by famous artists and by those long neglected outside Spain's borders. Gifts and an active acquisition policy have substantially enlarged the core collections of works by court artists and of paintings from the Trinity Museum. The Prado is the temple of Diego Velázquez and Francisco de Goya, and it also possesses important canvases by El Greco, Bartolomé Esteban Murillo, and Francisco de Zurbarán. Priceless medieval mural paintings—elements from the Mozarabic church of San Baudelio in Casillas de Berlanga and from the Santa Cruz Hermitage in Maderuelo, Segovia—complement the Prado's collection of Primitives, which is dominated by the imposing *Retable of Archbishop Don Sancho de Rojas* by Rodriguez de Toledo(?). Such important works from late fifteenth-century Castile as the *Pietà* by Fernando Gallego and portions of Pedro Berruguete's altarpiece for the Convent of Saint Thomas in Avila arrived at the Prado via monasteries and convents. There are also panels from Aragón, Valencia, and Catalonia representing the schools of those regions.

Though less rich in items from Andalusia, the Prado offers a superb overview of the Spanish Renaissance: works by the Italian-influenced Valencian painter Vicente Masip, Mannerist exercises like *The Descent from the Cross* by Pedro Machuca (who designed Charles V's palace in Granada), and thirty paintings by Luis de Morales. The last-named constitute a comprehensive sampling of works by Morales, who, like El Greco, moved from Crete to Toledo and was influenced by the Counter-Reformation. The final phase of Morales' career is especially well represented at the Prado because later acquisitions have supplemented his portraits from the royal collections and his important canvases from convents in the Madrid region.

The establishment of the Trinity Museum and the active patronage of Philip IV resulted in a spectacular stronghold of seventeenth-century works. Velázquez's youth in Seville is represented by two paintings, *The Adoration of the Magi* and his portrait of Sor Jerónima de la Fuente; more than forty works, including landscapes, mythological scenes, and portraits of kings and dwarfs, attest to his activity at court, which culminated in his elaborate masterpiece, *Las Meninas*.

Velázquez was, of course, not the only artist working in Madrid. Paintings by Juan Bautista Maino, Francisco de Herrera the Younger, and Juan Carreño de Miranda, to

name only three, reveal the obvious influence of their Flemish and Italian contemporaries. The recently acquired *Still Life with Game, Fruit, and Vegetables* by Juan Sánchez Cotán and a still life by Zurbarán exemplify the indigenous tradition of this genre.

The Prado has also obtained important works by the leading figures of Andalusian painting—Murillo, Alonso Cano, and Zurbarán—all of whom resided in the capital during the seventeenth century. Some canvases by Murillo came from the royal collections, at the bequest of Isabella Farnese; others (*The Soult Immaculate Conception* and the *Foundation of Santa Maria Maggiore in Rome*) entered the collection due to the vicissitudes of the Napoleonic wars. Most of the paintings by Jusepe de Ribera, who is extremely well represented, are of royal provenance, having arrived via the collection of the Viceroy of Naples.

Painting in eighteenth-century Spain was dominated first by French and Italian influences and later by Goya. Notable works from this period include Luis Eugenio Meléndez's remarkable series of still lifes from the Aranjuez palace, Luis Paret y Alcázar's idiosyncratic inflections of the French rococo style, and the Bayeu brothers' numerous cartoons for the tapestry factory of Santa Barbara.

Twenty-five works by Goya offer magnificent examples of every aspect of his career: tapestry cartoons for the royal apartments; portraits of the royal family and members of the aristocracy; the two *Majas*; his incomparable visions of the Peninsular War; and his enigmatic compositions for the Quinta del Sordo, his penultimate residence: dark paintings combining violence, witchcraft, historical drama, and psychological agony. In addition, the Prado has a magisterial ensemble of some five hundred drawings by Goya representing every phase of his career, from the Sanlucar albums (1797) and those of the Madrid period (which contain many preparatory drawings for prints) to Los Caprichos and the epic Disasters of War series. The Prado also owns several of his bullfights and Proverbs, as well as some of the artist's last sheets, produced during his exile in Bordeaux.

Eclecticism dominates the nineteenth-century works in the Casón del Buen Retiro. Portraits by Vicente Lopez are succeeded by the great historical canvases of Antonio Gisbert and Francisco Pradilla, by various examples of *costumbrismo* (depictions of typical scenes from Spanish life), and by a broad range of Spanish landscape painting gathered around a core of works by Aureliano de Beruete, Joaquín Sorolla, and Santiago Rusiñol.

Mural Paintings from the Santa Cruz Hermitage in Maderuelo, Segovia,
12th century. Fresco transferred to canvas,
room size: 16⅜ x 14¾ ft. (5 x 4.5 m.)

RODRÍGUEZ DE TOLEDO(?) (active 1st half of 15th century)
Retable of Archbishop Don Sancho de Rojas, c. 1414–22
Tempera on panel, 16⅞ x 11½ ft. (5 x 3.5 m.)

NICOLAS FRANCÉS (active 1434–1468)
Retable of the Life of the Virgin and of Saint Francis, c. 1455–60
Tempera on panel, 19⅝ x 19⅝ ft. (5.6 x 5.6 m.)

26

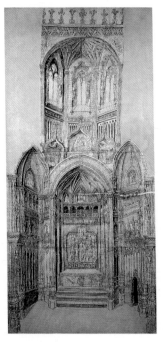

JUAN GUAS (active 1453–96)
The Main Chapel of San Juan de los Reyes in Toledo, n.d.
Ink on parchment, 76⅜ x 37¾ in. (194 x 96 cm)   27

FERNANDO GALLEGO (active 1466–1507)
Pietà, c. 1470
Tempera on panel, 49¼ x 42⅞ in. (125 x 109 cm)

FERNANDO GALLEGO (active 1466–1507)
The Martyrdom of Saint Catherine, n.d.
Tempera on panel, 49¼ x 42⅞ in. (125 x 109 cm)   29

MASTER OF MIRAFLORES (active 2d half of 15th century)
The Virgin of the Catholic Kings, c. 1490
Oil on panel, 48⅜ x 44⅛ in. (123 x 112 cm)

HISPANO–FLEMISH SCHOOL
Virgin in Prayer, 15th century
Alabaster

PEDRO BERRUGUETE (c. 1450–1503)
The Virgin Appearing to a Community of Dominicans, c. 1490–99
Oil on panel, 51¼ x 33⅜ in. (130 x 86 cm)

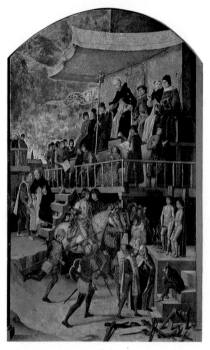

PEDRO BERRUGUETE (c. 1450–1503)
Saint Dominic Presiding over an Auto-da-fé, c. 1495
Oil on panel, 60⅜ x 38¼ in. (154 x 92 cm)

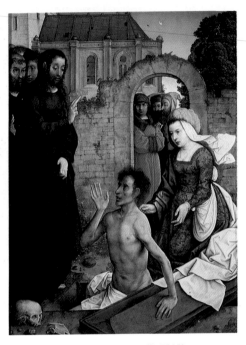

JUAN DE FLANDES (?–1519)
The Resurrection of Lazarus, c. 1512–18
Oil on panel, 48⅜ x 33⅛ in. (110 x 84 cm)

PABLO DE SAN LEOCADIO (active end of 15th century)
The Virgin with a Knight of Montesa, c. 1473–76
Oil on panel, 40¼ x 37¾ in. (102 x 96 cm)

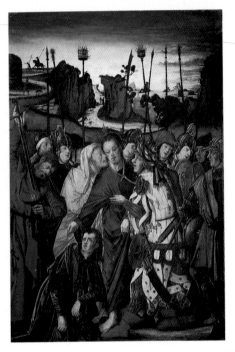

RODRIGO DE OSONA THE YOUNGER (active 1496–1510)
The Taking of Christ, n.d.
Oil on panel, 49⅝ x 33⅛ in. (126 x 84 cm)

ALEJO FERNÁNDEZ (c. 1475–1545)
The Flagellation of Christ, n.d.
Oil(?) on panel, 16½ x 13¾ in. (42 x 35 cm)

VICENTE MASIP (c. 1475–1545)
The Martyrdom of Saint Agnes, c. 1540
Oil on panel, diameter: 22¾ in. (58 cm)

FERNANDO YÁÑEZ DE LA ALMEDINA (c. 1489–1536)
Saint Catherine, n.d.
Oil on panel, 83½ x 44⅛ in. (212 x 112 cm)

PEDRO MACHUCA (c. 1490–1550)
The Descent from the Cross, 1547(?)
Oil on panel, 55½ x 50⅜ in. (141 x 128 cm)

JUAN DE JUANES (before 1523–1579)
The Last Supper, c. 1560
Oil on panel, 45⅝ x 75¼ in. (116 x 191 cm)

JUAN CORREA DE VIVAR (c. 1510–1566)
The Death of the Virgin, c. 1545–50
Oil on panel, 100 x 57⅞ in. (254 x 147 cm)

LUIS DE MORALES (c. 1515–1586)
The Virgin and Child, n.d.
Oil on panel, 33⅛ x 25¼ in. (84 x 64 cm)

LUIS DE MORALES (c. 1515–1586)
The Presentation of the Young Jesus in the Temple, n.d.
Oil on panel, 57½ x 44⅞ in. (146 x 114 cm)

ALONSO SÁNCHEZ COELLO (1531/32–1588)
The Infantas Isabella Clara Eugenia and Catalina Micaela, c. 1575
Oil on canvas, 53⅛ x 58⅝ in. (135 x 149 cm)   45

EL GRECO (1541–1614)
Portrait of a Man with His Hand on His Chest, c. 1577–79
Oil on canvas, 31⅞ x 26 in. (81 x 66 cm)

EL GRECO (1541–1614)
The Trinity, 1577–79
Oil on canvas, 118⅛ x 70½ in. (300 x 179 cm)   47

EL GRECO (1541–1614)
Rodrigo de la Fuente, Doctor, c. 1585–89
Oil on canvas, 36⅝ x 32⅜ in. (93 x 82 cm)

El Greco (1541–1614)
The Coronation of the Virgin, c. 1590–95
Oil on canvas, 35⅜ x 39⅜ in. (90 x 100 cm)

E L G RECO (1541–1614)
Saint Andrew and Saint Francis, c. 1590–95
Oil on canvas, 65⅜ x 44½ in. (167 x 113 cm)

EL GRECO (1541–1614)
The Annunciation, 1596–1600
Oil on canvas, 124⅜ x 68½ in. (316 x 174 cm)

EL GRECO (1541–1614)
Christ Carrying the Cross, c. 1600–1605
Oil on canvas, 42½ x 30⅜ in. (108 x 78 cm)

EL GRECO (1541–1614)
The Adoration of the Shepherds, c. 1603–14
Oil on canvas, 125⅜ x 70⅞ in. (319 x 180 cm)

EL GRECO (1541–1614)
Saint Sebastian, c. 1610–14
Oil on canvas, 49⅜ x 33½ in. (115 x 85 cm)

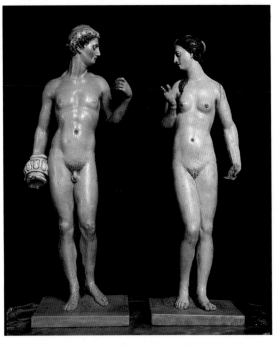

El Greco (1541–1614)
Epimetheus and Pandora, n.d.
Polychrome wood, height: 16⅞ in. (43 cm)

JUAN PANTOJA DE LA CRUZ (1553–1608)
Margaret of Austria, Queen of Spain, 1606
Oil on canvas, 80⅜ x 48 in. (204 x 122 cm)

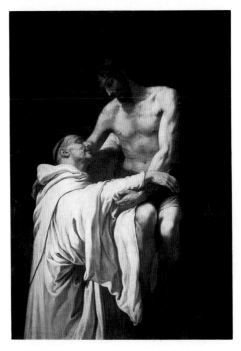

FRANCISCO RIBALTA (1565–1628)
Christ Embracing Saint Bernard, 1621–25
Oil on canvas, 62¼ x 44½ in. (158 x 113 cm)

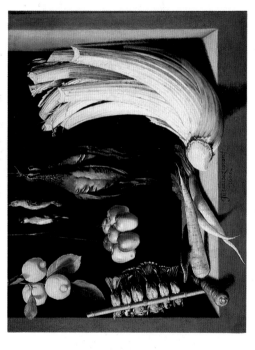

JUAN SÁNCHEZ COTÁN (1560–1627)
Still Life with Game, Fruit, and Vegetables, 1622
Oil on canvas, 27¼ x 34⅝ in. (69 x 88 cm)

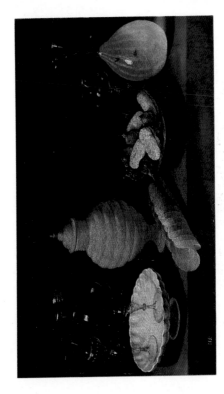

JUAN VAN DER HAMEN (1596–1631)
Still Life with Sweets and Glassware, 1622
Oil on canvas, 20½ x 34⅜ in. (52 x 88 cm)

JUAN BAUTISTA MAINO (1581–1649)
The Recapture of Bahia in 1625, 1634–35
Oil on canvas, 10⅛ x 12½ ft. (3.1 x 3.8 m.)

JUSEPE DE RIBERA (1591–1652)
Head of a Warrior, n.d. Red chalk on cream paper,
7⅞ x 10⅜ in. (20.2 x 26.5 cm)

JUSEPE DE RIBERA (1591–1652)
The Trinity, c. 1635–36
Oil on canvas, 92⅞ x 71⅜ in. (226 x 181 cm)

JUSEPE DE RIBERA (1591–1652)
Women Fighting, 1636
Oil on canvas, 92½ x 83½ in. (235 x 212 cm)

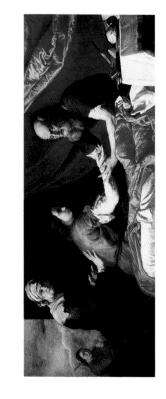

JUSEPE DE RIBERA (1591–1652)
The Blessing of Jacob, 1637
Oil on canvas, 50⅝ x 113¾ in. (129 x 289 cm)

JUSEPE DE RIBERA (1591–1652)
Jacob's Dream, 1639
Oil on canvas, 70½ x 91⅜ in. (179 x 233 cm)

JUSEPE DE RIBERA (1591–1652)
The Martyrdom of Saint Philip, 1639
Oil on canvas, 92⅛ x 92⅛ in. (234 x 234 cm)

JUSEPE DE RIBERA (1591–1652)
The Penitent Saint Jerome, 1652
Oil on canvas, 30⅜ x 28 in. (77 x 71 cm)

FRANCISCO DE ZURBARÁN (1598–1664)
The Defense of Cádiz Against the English, 1634
Oil on canvas, 119⅝ x 127¼ in. (304 x 323 cm)

FRANCISCO DE ZURBARÁN (1598–1664)
Still Life, c. 1635–40
Oil on canvas, 15⅛ x 33⅜ in. (46 x 84 cm)

FRANCISCO DE ZURBARÁN (1598–1664)
The Immaculate Conception, c. 1630
Oil on canvas, 54⅜ x 40⅞ in. (139 x 104 cm)

FRANCISCO DE ZURBARÁN (1598–1664)
Saint Euphemia, c. 1635–40
Oil on canvas, 32⅝ x 28⅜ in. (83 x 73 cm)

FRANCISCO DE ZURBARÁN (1598–1664)
Salvator Mundi, 1638
Oil on canvas, 39⅜ x 28⅜ in. (100 x 72 cm)

DIEGO VELÁZQUEZ (1599–1660)
The Adoration of the Magi, 1619
Oil on canvas, 80 x 49¼ in. (203 x 125 cm)

DIEGO VELÁZQUEZ (1599–1660)
Infante Don Carlos, c. 1626–27
Oil on canvas, 82⅜ x 49¼ in. (209 x 125 cm)

DIEGO VELÁZQUEZ (1599–1660)
Balthasar Carlos on Horseback, 1635–36
Oil on canvas, 82⅜ x 68⅛ in. (209 x 173 cm)

DIEGO VELÁZQUEZ (1599–1660)
The Triumph of Bacchus (The Drinkers), 1628
Oil on canvas, 65 x 88⅝ in. (165 x 225 cm)

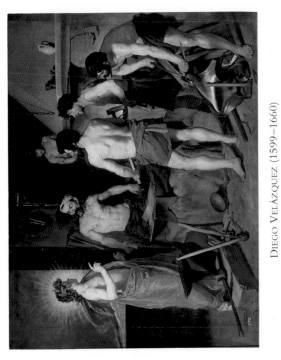

DIEGO VELÁZQUEZ (1599–1660)
Vulcan's Forge, 1630
Oil on canvas, 87¾ x 114¼ in. (223 x 290 cm)

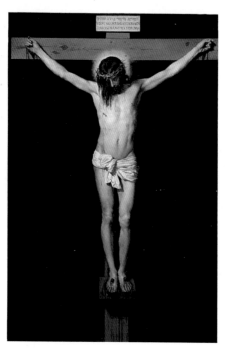

Diego Velázquez (1599–1660)
Christ on the Cross, c. 1632
Oil on canvas, 97⅜ x 66½ in. (248 x 169 cm)

DIEGO VELÁZQUEZ (1599–1660)
The Jester Known as "Don Juan de Austria," c. 1634–36
Oil on canvas, 82⅜ x 49⅜ in. (210 x 123 cm)

DIEGO VELÁZQUEZ (1599–1660)
Aesop, 1640
Oil on canvas, 70½ x 37 in. (179 x 94 cm)

DIEGO VELÁZQUEZ (1599–1660)
Mars, c. 1640
Oil on canvas, 70½ x 37⅜ in. (179 x 95 cm)

DIEGO VELÁZQUEZ (1599–1660)
The Surrender of Breda, 1635
Oil on canvas, 10 x 12 ft. (3.1 x 3.7 m.)

DIEGO VELÁZQUEZ (1599–1660)
The Coronation of the Virgin, c. 1641–44
Oil on canvas, 69⅜ x 48¾ in. (176 x 124 cm)

DIEGO VELÁZQUEZ (1599–1660)
Diego de Acedo, "El Primo," 1644
Oil on canvas, 41⅜ x 31⅞ in. (106 x 81 cm)

DIEGO VELÁZQUEZ (1599–1660)
The Medici Gardens in Rome, c. 1650–51
Oil on canvas, 18⅞ x 16½ in. (48 x 42 cm)

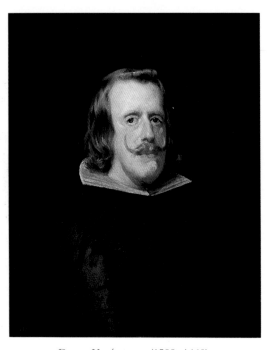

DIEGO VELÁZQUEZ (1599–1660)
Philip IV, c. 1653–55
Oil on canvas, 27¼ x 22 in. (69 x 56 cm)

DIEGO VELÁZQUEZ (1599–1660)
Las Meninas, 1656
Oil on canvas, 125¼ x 108⅜ in. (318 x 276 cm)

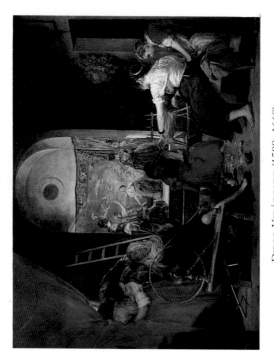

DIEGO VELÁZQUEZ (1599–1660)
The Spinners (The Fable of Arachne), c. 1657
Oil on canvas, 86⅝ x 113¾ in. (220 x 289 cm)

DIEGO VELÁZQUEZ (1599–1660)
Mercury and Argus, 1659
Oil on canvas, 50 x 97⅞ in. (127 x 248 cm)

ALONSO CANO (1601–1667)
The Dead Christ Supported by an Angel, c. 1646–52
Oil on canvas, 70⅛ x 47⅝ in. (178 x 121 cm)

ALONSO CANO (1601–1667)
The Annunciation, 1645(?). Brown ink and sepia wash
on cream paper, 10¼ x 6½ in. (26 x 17.6 cm)

JUAN BAUTISTA MARTÍNEZ DEL MAZO (c. 1610/15–1667)
View of Saragossa, 1646
Oil on canvas, 71⅜ x 130⅜ in. (181 x 331 cm)

ANTONIO DE PEREDA (1611–1678)
The Relief of Genoa, 1634–35
Oil on canvas, 9½ x 12⅛ ft. (2.9 x 3.7 m.)

JUAN DE ARELLANO (1614–1676)
Garland of Flowers with Landscape, 1652
Oil on canvas, 22¾ x 28⅝ in. (58 x 73 cm)

JUAN CARREÑO DE MIRANDA (1614–1685)
Charles II, c. 1675–76
Oil on canvas, 79⅛ x 55½ in. (201 x 141 cm)   95

JUAN CARREÑO DE MIRANDA (1614–1685)
Piotr Ivanowitz Potemkin, the Russian Ambassador, 1681–82
Oil on canvas, 80⅜ x 47¼ in. (204 x 120 cm)

JUAN CARREÑO DE MIRANDA (1614–1685)
Nude Christ, n.d. Black and red chalk on gray-beige paper,
16½ x 9⅛ in. (42 x 23 cm)

FRANCISCO RIZI (1614–1685)
Auto-da-fé on the Plaza Mayor in Madrid, 1683
Oil on canvas, 9⅛ x 14⅜ ft. (2.8 x 4.4 m.)

FRANCISCO DE HERRERA THE YOUNGER (1622–1685)
The Triumph of Saint Hermengild, 1654
Oil on canvas, 129⅛ x 90¼ in. (328 x 229 cm)

CLAUDIO COELLO (1642–1693)
The Triumph of Saint Augustine, 1664
Oil on canvas, 106⅜ x 79⅞ in. (271 x 203 cm)

CLAUDIO COELLO (1642–1693)
Saint Rose of Lima, c. 1684–85
Oil on canvas, 94½ x 63 in. (240 x 160 cm)

BARTOLOMÉ ESTEBAN MURILLO (1618–1682)
The Holy Family with a Bird, c. 1650
Oil on canvas, 56⅝ x 74 in. (144 x 188 cm)

BARTOLOMÉ ESTEBAN MURILLO (1618–1682)
Saint Anne and the Virgin, c. 1665
Oil on canvas, 86¼ x 65 in. (219 x 165 cm)

BARTOLOMÉ ESTEBAN MURILLO (1618–1682)
The Virgin Descending to Reward Saint Ildefonso, c. 1660
Oil on canvas, 121⅜ x 99⅜ in. (309 x 251 cm)

BARTOLOMÉ ESTEBAN MURILLO (1618–1682)
The Soult Immaculate Conception, c. 1678
Oil on canvas, 106⅞ x 74¾ in. (274 x 190 cm)

BARTOLOMÉ ESTEBAN MURILLO (1618–1682)
*The Foundation of Santa Maria Maggiore in Rome:
The Patrician's Dream*, c. 1662–65

BARTOLOMÉ ESTEBAN MURILLO (1618–1682)
The Holy Children with Shell, c. 1678
Oil on canvas, 40⅞ x 48¾ in. (104 x 124 cm)

JUAN DE VALDÉS LEAL (1622–1690)
Jesus among the Doctors, 1686
Oil on canvas, 78⅜ x 84⅝ in. (200 x 215 cm)

LUIS EUGENIO MELÉNDEZ (1716–1780)
Still Life with Box of Sweets, 1770
Oil on canvas, 19⅜ x 14⅝ in. (49 x 37 cm)

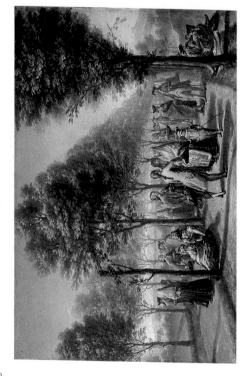

FRANCISCO BAYEU (1734–1795)
The Paseo de las Delicias in Madrid, 1785
Oil on canvas, 14⅝ x 21⅝ in. (37 x 55 cm)

FRANCISCO BAYEU (1734–1795)
Olympus: The Fall of the Giants, 1764
Design for ceiling of the Royal Palace, 26⅞ x 48⅜ in. (68 x 123 cm)

José del Castillo (1737–1793)
The Painter's Studio, 1780
Oil on canvas, 39⅜ x 62⅝ in. (100 x 159 cm)

RAMÓN BAYEU (1746–1793)
Boy with Guitar, c. 1786
Oil on canvas, 72⅜ x 53⅞ in. (184 x 137 cm)

VICENTE LOPEZ (1772–1850)
Francisco de Goya, 1826
Oil on canvas, 36⅝ x 29½ in. (93 x 75 cm)

FRANCISCO DE GOYA (1746–1828)
A Dance at San Antonio de la Florida, 1777
Oil on canvas, 107⅛ x 116⅛ in. (272 x 295 cm)

FRANCISCO DE GOYA (1746–1828)
The Parasol, 1777
Oil on canvas, 40⅞ x 59⅝ in. (104 x 152 cm)

FRANCISCO DE GOYA (1746–1828)
The Pottery Vendor, 1779
Oil on canvas, 102 x 86⅝ in. (259 x 220 cm)

FRANCISCO DE GOYA (1746–1828)
Winter (The Snowstorm), 1786
Oil on canvas, 108⅜ x 115⅜ in. (275 x 293 cm)

FRANCISCO DE GOYA (1746–1828)
The Meadow of San Isidro, 1788
Oil on canvas, 17⅞ x 37 in. (44 x 94 cm)

FRANCISCO DE GOYA (1746–1828)
The Family of the Duke of Osuna, 1788
Oil on canvas, 88⅝ x 68½ in. (225 x 174 cm)

FRANCISCO DE GOYA (1746–1828)
Charles IV and His Family, 1800
Oil on canvas, 110¼ x 132⅜ in. (280 x 336 cm)

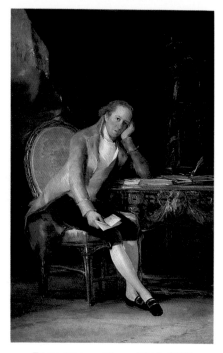

FRANCISCO DE GOYA (1746–1828)
Gaspar Melchor de Jovellanos, 1797
Oil on canvas, 80⅜ x 43⅜ in. (205 x 123 cm)

FRANCISCO DE GOYA (1746–1828)
I Am Still Learning (Album G, 54), 1824–28
Black chalk on paper, 7½ x 5⅝ in. (19.1 x 14.6 cm)   123

FRANCISCO DE GOYA (1746–1828)
The Duchess of Alba and the Young Maria de la Luz, 1797
Brown ink on cream paper, 6½ x 4 in. (16.5 x 9 cm)

FRANCISCO DE GOYA (1746–1828)
Title Page for "Dreams," 2d Version, 1797. Pen and sepia ink over charcoal on paper, 9 x 5⅞ in. (22.8 x 15.1 cm)   125

Francisco de Goya (1746–1828)
The Literate Ass, from Los Caprichos, 1797–98
126 Pen and sepia ink on paper, 9 x 6¾ in. (22.8 x 17.2 cm)

FRANCISCO DE GOYA (1746–1828)
That Dust, from Los Caprichos, 1797–98. Red chalk and
sanguine wash on paper, 7⅞ x 45⅛ in. (20 x 114.6 cm)   127

Francisco de Goya (1746–1828)
Nude Maja, before November 1800
Oil on canvas, 37⅜ x 74¾ in. (95 x 190 cm)

FRANCISCO DE GOYA (1746–1828)
Clothed Maja, c. 1800–1803
Oil on canvas, 37⅜ x 74¾ in. (95 x 190 cm)

Francisco de Goya (1746–1828)
The Second of May, 1808, 1814
Oil on canvas, 104⅝ x 135¾ in. (266 x 345 cm)

FRANCISCO DE GOYA (1746–1828)
The Third of May, 1808, 1814
Oil on canvas, 104⅝ x 135⅞ in. (266 x 345 cm)

FRANCISCO DE GOYA (1746–1828)
Because He Has No Work (Album C, I), 1808–10
132   India ink wash on paper, 8⅛ x 5⅝ in. (20.5 x 14.4 cm)

FRANCISCO DE GOYA (1746–1828)
For Being a Liberal? (Album C, 98), 1808–10
Sepia wash on paper, 8⅛ x 5¾ in. (20.5 x 14.3 cm)

FRANCISCO DE GOYA (1746–1828)
What Courage! from The Disasters of War, c. 1810–15
Red chalk on paper, 5⅝ x 7¾ in. (14.5 x 19.8 cm)

FRANCISCO DE GOYA (1746–1828)
The Famous Fernando del Toro Keeping the Beast at Bay with His Pike,
from *Tauromachia*, 1815–16. Red chalk and sanguine wash
on paper, 7⅜ x 12½ in. (18.7 x 31.7 cm)

Francisco de Goya (1746–1828)
Duel with Cudgels, c. 1819–23
Oil on canvas, 49⅜ x 104⅝ in. (123 x 266 cm)

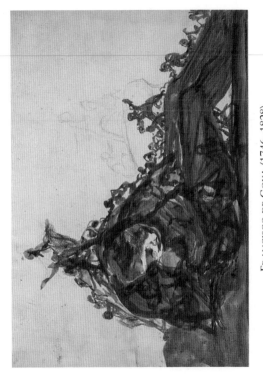

FRANCISCO DE GOYA (1746–1828)
Figures Clambering over a Reclining Giant, c. 1815–24
Red wash on paper, 9¼ x 9⅜ in. (23.4 x 23.8 cm)

FRANCISCO DE GOYA (1746–1828)
Ferdinand VII in His Robes of State, 1814
Oil on canvas, 83½ x 57½ in. (212 x 146 cm)

FRANCISCO DE GOYA (1746–1828)
Saturn Devouring One of His Sons, c. 1819–23
Oil on canvas, 57½ x 32⅝ in. (146 x 83 cm)

LUIS PARET Y ALCÁZAR (1746–1799)
Charles III Lunching before His Court, c. 1768–73
Oil on panel, 19⅝ x 25¼ in. (50 x 64 cm)

LUIS PARET Y ALCÁZAR (1746–1799)
The Rehearsal, c. 1772–73
Oil on canvas, 15 x 20½ in. (38 x 51 cm)

ANTONIO CARNICERO (1748–1814)
Balloon Ascent at Aranjuez, 1784
Oil on canvas, 66⅞ x 111¾ in. (170 x 284 cm)

JOSÉ DE MADRAZO (1781–1859)
The Death of Viriathus, c. 1818
Oil on canvas, 10⅛ x 15⅝ ft. (3.1 x 4.6 m.)

ANTONIO MARÍA ESQUIVEL (1806–1857)
Gathering of Poets, 1846
Oil on canvas, 56⅝ x 84¼ in. (144 x 214 cm)

BERNARDO LOPEZ (1801–1874)
Isabella of Braganza, Second Wife of Ferdinand VII, 1829
Oil on canvas, 60⅝ x 67⅞ in. (154 x 172 cm)   145

FEDERICO DE MADRAZO (1815–1894)
The Countess of Vilches, 1853
Oil on canvas, 49⅝ x 35 in. (126 x 89 cm)

EUGENIO LUCAS VELÁZQUEZ (1817–1870)
The Presidents, n.d.
Oil on canvas, 28⅜ x 21⅝ in. (72 x 55 cm)

ANTONIO GISBERT (1834–1901)
The Execution of Torrijos and His Companions, c. 1886–88
Oil on canvas, 12¾ x 19⅝ ft. (3.9 x 6 m.)

EDUARDO ROSALES (1836–1873)
The Testament of Isabella the Catholic, 1864
Oil on canvas, 9½ x 13⅜ ft. (2.9 x 4 m.)

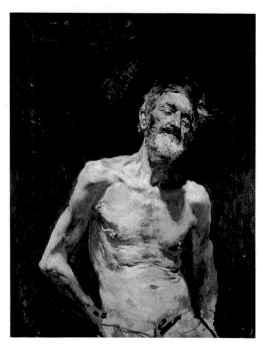

MARIANO FORTUNY (1838–1874)
Nude Old Man in the Sun, c. 1873
Oil on canvas, 32⅝ x 22¾ in. (83 x 58 cm)

IGNAZIO PINAZO (1849–1916)
Self-Portrait, 1895
Oil on canvas, 32⅝ x 24 in. (83 x 61 cm)

FRANCISCO PRADILLA (1848–1921)
Jean the Mad, 1877
Oil on canvas, 11¼ x 16⅜ ft. (3.4 x 5 m.)

SANTIAGO RUSIÑOL (1861–1931)
The Garden of Aranjuez, 1908
Oil on canvas, 55⅛ x 52¾ in. (140 x 134 cm)

DARIO DE REGOYOS (1857–1913)
The San Sebastián Beach, n.d.
Oil on canvas, 11¾ x 16⅛ in. (30 x 41 cm)

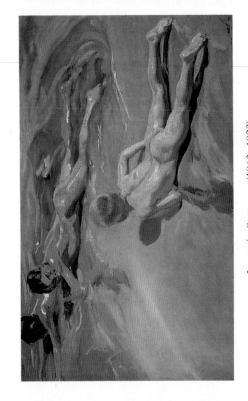

JOAQUÍN SOROLLA (1863–1923)
Little Boys on the Beach, 1910
Oil on canvas, 32⅜ x 58⅝ in. (82 x 149 cm)

FLEMISH AND DUTCH PAINTING

The Prado's Flemish collection is exceptional in both quality and breadth. This superb ensemble comes in large part from the royal collections accumulated since the reign of Charles V, and its quality is intimately linked to historical circumstances. Close economic ties between Flanders and Spain from the fifteenth century onward led to an influx of works that left a Flemish imprint on contemporary Spanish production. The monarchs' political relationships and personal tastes favored the subsequent development of this interest, which culminated in multiple commissions for works by Peter Paul Rubens. (Recent acquisitions have led to a better representation of sixteenth-century Flemish art, even strengthening the already strong collection of Rubens.) In the eighteenth century the Bourbons prolonged this tradition by acquiring genre scenes by David Teniers and others.

The early Flemish masters are represented with magisterial works: *The Descent from the Cross* is surely Rogier van der Weyden's masterpiece, and Robert Campin's panels *Saint Barbara* and *Saint John the Baptist* are of superb quality. Philip II was a passionate collector of Flemish painting. He purchased portraits by Antonio Moro, landscapes by Joachim Patinir, and above all, works by Hieronymus Bosch that constitute the greatest ensemble of works by that master in a single museum.

Rubens is represented in the Prado by some sixty works derived from his two sojourns in Spain and his great decorative commissions for Philip IV. Upon the painter's death Philip IV acquired *The Three Graces, Perseus and Andromeda,* and other of his works. This extraordinary wealth of paintings by Rubens, however, should not overshadow the Prado's battle paintings by Pieter Snayers, allegories by Jan Brueghel the Elder, and important canvases by Anthony Van Dyck, such as *Sir Endymion Porter and Van Dyck,* acquired in the eighteenth century.

The prolonged rebellion of the northern Low Countries led to the establishment of the United Provinces in 1648; the adversarial relations between that country and Spain explain the absence of Dutch works in the royal collections prior to the eighteenth century. Isabella Farnese, however, acquired genre paintings by Adriaen van Ostade and Philips Wouwerman; Charles III bought the Prado's only Rembrandt, the magnificent *Artemisia;* and Charles IV acquired *Dead Rooster,* one of Gabriel Metsu's finest still lifes. As a result of subsequent acquisitions and donations the Prado's range of seventeenth-century Dutch painting is comprehensive, despite the absence of works by Jan Vermeer and Frans Hals.

ROBERT CAMPIN (1378/79–1444)
Saint John the Baptist and the Franciscan Heinrich Werl, 1438
Oil on panel, 39¾ x 18½ in. (101 x 47 cm)

ROBERT CAMPIN (1378/79–1444)
Saint Barbara, 1438
Oil on panel, 39¾ x 18½ in. (101 x 47 cm)   161

ROGIER VAN DER WEYDEN (1399/1400–1464)
The Descent from the Cross, c. 1435
162   Oil on panel, 86⅝ x 103⅛ in. (220 x 262 cm)

ROGIER VAN DER WEYDEN (1399/1400–1464)
The Virgin and Child, c. 1436/38
Oil on panel, 39⅜ x 20½ in. (100 x 52 cm)

Rogier van der Weyden (1399/1400–1464)
Pietà, c. 1450
Oil on panel, 18½ x 13¾ in. (47 x 35 cm)

SCHOOL OF VAN EYCK
The Fountain of Grace, c. 1455–59
Oil on panel, 71¼ x 45⅝ in. (181 x 116 cm)

166

PETRUS CHRISTUS (1415/20–1472/73)
The Virgin and Child, c. 1457–60
Oil on panel, 19⅜ x 13⅜ in. (49 x 34 cm)

La Annunciation   La Visitation

168

DIRCK BOUTS (c. 1420–1475). *The Annunciation, Visitation,*
Adoration of the Angels, Adoration of the Magi, c. 1445
Oil on panel, 31½ x 124 in. (80 x 217 cm), overall 169

Hans Memling (c. 1433/35–1494)
The Nativity, Adoration of the Magi, Purification, c. 1470
Oil on panel, 37⅛ x 106¾ in. (95 x 271 cm), overall   171

HIERONYMUS BOSCH (c. 1450–1516)
The Table of the Seven Deadly Sins, c. 1480
Oil on panel, 47¼ x 59⅛ in. (120 x 150 cm)

HIERONYMUS BOSCH (c. 1450–1516)
The Hay Wagon, c. 1495–1500
Oil on panel, 53⅛ x 74½ in. (135 x 190 cm), overall

HIERONYMUS BOSCH (c. 1450–1516)
The Garden of Delights, c. 1506–16
Oil on panel, 86⅜ x 153 in. (220 x 389 cm), overall   177

HIERONYMUS BOSCH (c. 1450–1516)
The Adoration of the Magi, c. 1510
Oil on panel, 54⅜ x 55¼ in. (138 x 140 cm), overall

GERARD DAVID (c. 1460–1523)
The Rest on the Flight to Egypt, c. 1515–23
Oil on panel, 23⅜ x 15⅜ in. (60 x 39 cm)

MABUSE (1470/80–1532)
The Virgin and Child, c. 1527
Oil on panel, 24¾ x 19⅝ in. (63 x 50 cm)

JOACHIM PATINIR (c. 1480–1524)
Charon Crossing the Styx, c. 1510
Oil on panel, 25¼ x 40⅝ in. (64 x 103 cm)

JOACHIM PATINIR (c. 1480–1524) and QUENTIN MASSYS (1465/66–1530)
The Temptation of Saint Anthony, before 1522
Oil on panel, 61 x 68⅛ in. (155 x 173 cm)

BERNAERDT VAN ORLEY (1488–1541)
The Holy Family, 1522
188   Oil on panel, 35⅜ x 29⅛ in. (90 x 74 cm)

MICHEL VAN COXCIE (1499–1592)
Saint Cecilia, c. 1569
Oil on panel, 53½ x 40⅞ in. (136 x 104 cm)

MARINUS VAN REYMERSWAELE (c. 1497– died after 1567?)
The Money Changer and His Wife, 1539
Oil on panel, 32⅝ x 38¼ in. (83 x 97 cm)

JAN SANDERS VAN HEMESSEN (c. 1500–c. 1564/66)
The Surgeon, c. 1550
Oil on panel, 39⅜ x 55½ in. (100 x 141 cm)

ANTONIO MORO (1517–1576)
Mary Tudor, Queen of England, 1554
Oil on panel, 42⅞ x 33⅛ in. (109 x 84 cm)

ANTONIO MORO (1517–1576)
Metgen, The Painter's Wife, c. 1554
Oil on panel, 39⅜ x 31½ in. (100 x 80 cm)

PIETER BRUEGHEL THE ELDER (c. 1520/30–1569)
The Triumph of Death, c. 1560
Oil on panel, 46⅛ x 63¾ in. (117 x 162 cm)

JAN BRUEGHEL THE ELDER (1568–1625)
and PETER PAUL RUBENS (1577–1640).
Allegory of Sight, 1617
Oil on panel, 25⅝ x 42⅞ in. (65 x 109 cm)

PETER PAUL RUBENS (1577–1640)
Saint George, 1606–7
Oil on canvas, 119⅝ x 100¾ in. (304 x 256 cm)

PETER PAUL RUBENS (1577–1640)
The Cardinal-Infante Don Fernando, 1634–35
Oil on canvas, 131⅞ x 101⅜ in. (335 x 258 cm)

PETER PAUL RUBENS (1577–1640)
The Triumph of the Church over Ignorance and Blindness, c. 1626
Oil on panel, 33⅞ x 41⅜ in. (86 x 105 cm)

PETER PAUL RUBENS (1577–1640)
The Garden of Love, c. 1633
Oil on canvas, 78 x 111⅜ in. (198 x 283 cm)

PETER PAUL RUBENS (1577–1640)
Atalanta and Meleager, before 1636
Oil on canvas, 63 x 102⅜ in. (160 x 260 cm)

PETER PAUL RUBENS (1577–1640)
Peasant Dance, c. 1636–40
Oil on panel, 28¾ x 41¾ in. (73 x 106 cm)

PETER PAUL RUBENS (1577–1640)
The Three Graces, c. 1636–38
Oil on panel, 87 x 71¼ in. (221 x 181 cm)

JACOB JORDAENS (1593–1678)
The Painter's Family, c. 1621–22
Oil on canvas, 71¼ x 73⅝ in. (181 x 187 cm)

JACOB JORDAENS (1593–1678)
Three Itinerant Musicians, n.d.
Oil on panel, 19⅜ x 25¼ in. (49 x 64 cm)

Anthony Van Dyck (1599–1641)
The Taking of Christ, c. 1618–20
Oil on canvas, 135⅜ x 98 in. (344 x 249 cm)

ANTHONY VAN DYCK (1599–1641)
Sir Endymion Porter and Van Dyck, c. 1632–1640
Oil on canvas, 43⅜ x 44¾ in. (110 x 114 cm)

ANTHONY VAN DYCK (1599–1641)
Maria Ruthwen, the Painter's Wife, c. 1639
Oil on canvas, 40⅞ x 31⅞ in. (104 x 81 cm)

ADRIAEN VAN OSTADE (1610–1684)
Peasants Singing, 1632
Oil on canvas, 9⅜ x 11⅜ in. (24 x 29 cm)

DAVID TENIERS THE YOUNGER (1610–1690)
Village Festival, 1647
Oil on canvas, 29½ x 44⅛ in. (75 x 112 cm)

PHILIPS WOUWERMAN (1619–1668)
Two Horses, n.d.
Oil on panel, 13 x 12⅝ in. (33 x 32 cm)

CLARA PEETERS (1594–1659)
Still Life, n.d.
Oil on panel, 21⅛ x 28⅝ in. (55 x 73 cm)

REMBRANDT VAN RIJN (1606–1669)
Artemisia, 1634
Oil on canvas, 56⅜ x 60¼ in. (143 x 153 cm)

ITALIAN PAINTING

The Italian holdings constitute the third largest in the Prado, comprising almost six hundred items, most of them from the royal collections. Like the Flemish works, these paintings reflect the predilections of the Spanish rulers, who were relatively unfamiliar with artists predating the High Renaissance; nonetheless, *The Annunciation* by Fra Angelico and *The Death of the Virgin* by Andrea Mantegna (the Prado's only work by this artist) were in the royal palace as early as the seventeenth century. In donating two works by Taddeo Gaddi and the three panels of Sandro Botticelli's *Story of Nastagio degli Onesti,* Francisco Cambó began the task of filling the gaps in the Italian collection, a project that has been carried forward with such acquisitions as Antonello da Messina's *Dead Christ Supported by an Angel.* The most impressive Italian ensemble is clearly that of Venetian sixteenth-century painting, dominated by Titian but also very rich in works by Tintoretto and Leandro Bassano.

As his grandfather had done for the Escorial, Philip IV commissioned numerous works from Italian artists for his palaces, above all the Buen Retiro. The *Triumphs* by Giovanni Lanfranco and assorted works by Domenichino and Guido Reni are only a handful among the many he acquired. Philip IV also revived a prestigious decorative tradition by employing Italian fresco painters, a policy continued by his son Charles II, who summoned Luca Giordano to oversee the decoration of his new palace in Madrid, on which Corrado Giaquinto, Anton Raphael Mengs, and Giambattista Tiepolo also worked. As a result, superb oil sketches by all of these artists remain in the Prado collections.

The marriage of Philip V to Isabella Farnese further strengthened the country's ties with Italy, which remained strong until the end of the eighteenth century—especially under Charles III, who was king of Naples before mounting the Spanish throne. Therefore, the Prado's enormous collection includes *vedute* (views) by Francesco Battaglioli; portraits by Jacopo Amigoni, Andrea Procaccini, and Giuseppe Bonito; still lifes by Mariano Nani; religious paintings by Francesco Trevisani; two portraits of elegant British gentlemen by Pompeo Gerolamo Batoni, which were acquired by Charles IV; and two Tiepolos. The canvases painted by Giambattista Tiepolo for the Church of San Pascual in Aranjuez (*The Immaculate Conception, The Triumph of Venus*) have a profound delicacy that sharply contrasts with the dramatic tone of the *Scenes from the Passion* by his son Gian Domenico.

FRA ANGELICO (c. 1400–1455)
The Annunciation, 1435–45

Tempera on panel, 76⅜ x 76⅜ in. (194 x 194 cm)

ANTONELLO DA MESSINA (c. 1430–1479)
Dead Christ Supported by an Angel, c. 1476–79
Oil on panel, 29⅛ x 20 in. (74 x 51 cm)

ANDREA MANTEGNA (1431–1506)
The Death of the Virgin, c. 1464
220   Tempera on panel, 21¼ x 16½ in. (54 x 42 cm)

Detail of Panel II of
The Story of Nastagio degli Onesti, 1482–83, by Sandro Botticelli
See page 223.

SANDRO BOTTICELLI (1445–1510)
Panel I of *The Story of Nastagio degli Onesti*, 1482–83
Tempera on panel, 32⅝ x 54⅜ in. (83 x 138 cm)

SANDRO BOTTICELLI (1445–1510)
Panel II of *The Story of Nastagio degli Onesti*, 1482–83
Tempera on panel, 32⅜ x 54⅜ in. (82 x 138 cm)

SANDRO BOTTICELLI (1445–1510)
Panel III of *The Story of Nastagio degli Onesti*, 1482–83
Tempera on panel, 33 x 54⅜ in. (84 x 138 cm)

GIOVANNI BELLINI (c. 1432–1516)
The Virgin and Child with Two Saints, c. 1490
Oil on panel, 30⅜ x 40⅞ in. (77 x 104 cm)

GIORGIONE (c. 1476/78–1510)
The Virgin and Child with Saint Anthony of Padua and Saint Roch, c. 1510(?)
Oil on canvas, 35¼ x 72 in. (92 x 183 cm)

RAPHAEL (1483–1520)
The Holy Family with a Lamb, 1507
Oil on panel, 11⅜ x 8¼ in. (29 x 21 cm)

Raphael (1483–1520)
Portrait of a Cardinal, c. 1510
Oil on panel, 31⅛ x 23⅝ in. (79 x 61 cm)

RAPHAEL (1483–1520)
The Madonna of the Fish, c. 1513. Oil on panel transferred
to canvas, 84⅜ x 62¼ in. (215 x 158 cm)

RAPHAEL (1483–1520)
Christ on the Way to Calvary, 1517. Oil on panel transferred
to canvas, 125¼ x 90¼ in. (318 x 229 cm)

SEBASTIANO DEL PIOMBO (c. 1485–1547)
Christ Carrying the Cross, c. 1520
Oil on canvas, 47⅜ x 39⅜ in. (121 x 100 cm)

ANDREA DEL SARTO (1486–1530)
Lucrezia di Baccio del Fede, the Painter's Wife, c. 1517
Oil on panel, 28¾ x 22 in. (73 x 56 cm)

ANDREA DEL SARTO (1486–1530)
The Virgin and Child with Tobias and the Archangel Raphael, c. 1515–20
Oil on panel, 69⅜ x 53⅛ in. (177 x 135 cm)

TITIAN (1488/90–1576)
The Worship of Venus, 1519
Oil on canvas, 67⅜ x 68⅞ in. (172 x 175 cm)

TITIAN (1488/90–1576)
Bacchanal, c. 1523–25
Oil on canvas, 68⅛ x 76 in. (175 x 193 cm)

TITIAN (1488/90–1576)
Alfonso d'Avalos Addressing His Troops, 1541
Oil on canvas, 87¾ x 65 in. (223 x 165 cm)

TITIAN (1488/90−1576)
The Emperor Charles V at Mühlberg, 1548
Oil on canvas, 130⅝ x 109⅝ in. (332 x 279 cm)   237

TITIAN (1488/90−1576)
Self-Portrait, 1566
Oil on canvas, 33⅞ x 25⅞ in. (86 x 65 cm)

TITIAN (1488/90–1576)
The Empress Isabella, Wife of Charles V, 1548
Oil on canvas, 46⅛ x 35⅜ in. (117 x 98 cm)

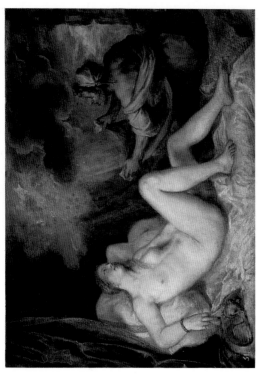

TITIAN (1488/90–1576)
Danaë and the Shower of Gold, 1553
Oil on canvas, 50½ x 70⅝ in. (129 x 180 cm)

TITIAN (1488/90–1576)
Spain Coming to the Aid of Religion, c. 1572–75
Oil on canvas, 66⅛ x 66⅛ in. (168 x 168 cm)

CORREGGIO (1489/94–1534)
Noli Me Tangere, c. 1525(?). Oil on panel transferred
to canvas, 51¼ x 40⅜ in. (130 x 103 cm)

AGNOLO BRONZINO (1503–1572)
Don Garcia de' Medici, c. 1550
Oil on panel, 18⅞ x 15 in. (48 x 38 cm)   243

PARMIGIANINO (1503–1540)
The Holy Family with an Angel, c. 1524
Oil on panel, 43⅜ x 35 in. (110 x 89 cm)

TINTORETTO (1518/19–1594)
Woman Revealing Her Breast, n.d.
Oil on canvas, 24 x 21⅛ in. (61 x 55 cm)

Tintoretto (1518/19–1594)
Christ Washing the Disciples' Feet, c. 1547
Oil on canvas, 6⅞ x 17½ ft. (2.1 x 5.3 m.)

TINTORETTO (1518/19–1594)
Esther and Ahasuerus, c. 1555
Oil on canvas, 23¼ x 79⅞ in. (59 x 203 cm)

FEDERIGO BAROCCI (1525/35–1612)
The Nativity, c. 1597
Oil on canvas, 52¾ x 41⅜ in. (134 x 105 cm)

PAOLO VERONESE (1528–1588)
The Finding of Moses, c. 1570–75
Oil on canvas, 19⅝ x 16⅞ in. (50 x 43 cm)

PAOLO VERONESE (1528–1588)
Christ and the Centurion, 1571
Oil on canvas, 75⅝ x 116⅞ in. (192 x 297 cm)

PAOLO VERONESE (1528–1588)
Venus and Adonis, c. 1580
Oil on canvas, 63⅞ x 75¼ in. (162 x 191 cm)

Annibale Carracci (1560–1609)
Venus, Adonis, and Cupid, c. 1590
Oil on canvas, 83½ x 105½ in. (212 x 268 cm)

CARAVAGGIO (1571–1610)
David and Goliath, n.d.
Oil on canvas, 43⅜ x 35¾ in. (110 x 91 cm)

GUIDO RENI (1575–1642)
Hipponenes and Atalanta, c. 1617–18
Oil on canvas, 81⅛ x 117 in. (206 x 297 cm)

MATTIA PRETI (1613–1699)
Christ in Glory with Saints, c. 1655
Oil on canvas, 86⅝ x 99⅝ in. (220 x 253 cm)

LUCA GIORDANO (1634–1705)
The Dream of Solomon, c. 1693
Oil on canvas, 96½ x 142⅛ in. (245 x 361 cm)

CORRADO GIAQUINTO (1703–1765/70)
Justice and Peace, c. 1754
Oil on canvas, 85 x 128 in. (216 x 325 cm)

GIAMBATTISTA TIEPOLO (1696–1770)
Abraham and the Three Angels, c. 1769
Oil on canvas, 77⅜ x 59⅜ in. (197 x 151 cm)

GIAMBATTISTA TIEPOLO (1696–1770)
The Immaculate Conception, 1769
Oil on canvas, 109⅝ x 59¾ in. (279 x 152 cm)

FRENCH, GERMAN,
AND ENGLISH PAINTING

Although less comprehensive than those of the Italian and
Flemish schools, the Prado's holdings in French painting
nevertheless feature some magnificent seventeenth-
century canvases, a taste stimulated by the Bourbons'
ascent to the Spanish throne in 1700. Most of this
ensemble came from the royal collections, although
certain recent acquisitions (*Vanitas* by Jacques Linard,
Hurdy-Gurdy Player with a Ribbon by Georges de La Tour)
have increased its scope.

In the seventeenth century, political pacts and
matrimonial alliances with France resulted in an exchange
of portraits between the two courts. The Prado therefore
owns beautiful works by Frans Pourbus, Charles
Beaubrun, and Pierre Mignard, plus Sébastien Bourdon's
extraordinary *Christina of Sweden on Horseback*. For the
Buen Retiro, Philip IV commissioned works from French
artists residing in Rome; a series of landscapes with
hermits includes canvases by Nicolas Poussin, Claude
Lorrain, and Gaspard Dughet. A few characteristic
paintings by Valentin (Jean de Boulogne), Nicolas
Tournier, and Simon Vouet also entered the museum via
the royal collections, and Philip V later acquired even

more French paintings: not only his portrait by Hyacinthe Rigaud but also portraits by Jean Ranc, Michel-Ange Houasse, and Louis-Michel van Loo, all of which betray the influence of Spanish art. Two paintings by Jean-Antoine Watteau, along with four landscapes by Joseph Vernet commissioned by Charles IV for the Casita at the Escorial, figure among the best works from France.

Very few German paintings made their way into the royal collections despite the title held by Charles V— Emperor of the Holy Roman Empire—and despite the extensive political and familial ties between Spain and the principalities that would later become Germany. The two *Hunts in Honor of Charles V at Torgau* by Lucas Cranach the Elder were certainly the first German works to enter the Prado. At the end of the eighteenth century the German-born painter Anton Raphael Mengs, an important theorist of Neoclassicism, resided in Madrid and became the dominant presence in its Academy. The Prado possesses a fine set of his portraits, remarkable for their elegance and technical virtuosity, as well as an *Adoration of the Shepherds* that evinces his admiration for Correggio. Philip II acquired the two allegories by Hans Baldung Grien (*Harmony, or the Three Graces* and *Death and the Ages of Man*), and Philip IV the four Dürers now in the Prado. Although the number of German works in the museum is small, they are of superb quality and illustrate the eclectic taste of these two great collectors.

A few acquisitions and donations have resulted in the Prado's owning a select number of eighteenth-century English works, and its gallery of portraits by Thomas Gainsborough, Joshua Reynolds, Henry Raeburn, and Thomas Lawrence is of considerable interest. Two Spanish landscapes by the Scotsman David Roberts remind us that the English Romantics harbored a passion for many things Iberian.

FRENCH PAINTING

SIMON VOUET (1590–1649)
Time Vanquished by Hope, Love, and Beauty, 1627
Oil on canvas, 42⅛ x 55⅝ in. (107 x 142 cm)

GEORGES DE LA TOUR (1593–1652)
Hurdy-Gurdy Player with a Ribbon, n.d.
Oil on canvas, 33⅛ x 24 in. (84 x 61 cm)

NICOLAS POUSSIN (1594–1665)
The Triumph of David, c. 1630–31
Oil on canvas, 39⅜ x 51¼ in. (100 x 130 cm)

NICOLAS POUSSIN (1594–1665)
Parnassus (Apollo and the Muses), c. 1631–33
Oil on canvas, 57⅛ x 77⅝ in. (145 x 197 cm)

CLAUDE LORRAIN (1600–1682)
Landscape with the Embarkation of Saint Paula Romana at Ostia, 1639
268   Oil on canvas, 83⅛ x 57⅛ in. (211 x 145 cm)

HYACINTHE RIGAUD (1659–1743)
Louis XIV, 1700
Oil on canvas, 93⅝ x 58⅜ in. (238 x 149 cm)

MICHEL-ANGE HOUASSE (1680–1730)
View of the Escorial Monastery, n.d.
Oil on canvas, 19⅝ x 32⅜ in. (50 x 82 cm)

JEAN-ANTOINE WATTEAU (1684–1721)
The Marriage Contract, c. 1712–16
Oil on canvas, 18½ x 21⅝ in. (47 x 55 cm)

LOUIS-MICHEL VAN LOO (1707–1771)
The Family of Philip V, 1743
Oil on canvas, 13⅜ x 16¾ ft. (4.1 x 5.1 m.)

GERMAN PAINTING

ALBRECHT DÜRER (1471–1528)
Self-Portrait, 1498
Oil on panel, 20½ x 16⅛ in. (52 x 41 cm)

ALBRECHT DÜRER (1471–1528)
Adam, 1507
Oil on panel, 82⅜ x 32¼ in. (209 x 81 cm)

ALBRECHT DÜRER (1471–1528)
Eve, 1507
Oil on panel, 82⅜ x 31½ in. (209 x 80 cm)

LUCAS CRANACH THE ELDER (1472–1553)
Hunt in Honor of Charles V at Torgau, 1544
Oil on panel, 44⅞ x 68⅜ in. (114 x 175 cm)

HANS BALDUNG GRIEN (1484/85–1545)
Death and the Ages of Man, 1540
Oil on panel, 59⅜ x 24 in. (151 x 61 cm)

ANTON RAPHAEL MENGS (1728–1779)
Charles III, 1761
Oil on canvas, 60⅜ x 43⅜ in. (154 x 110 cm)

ANTON RAPHAEL MENGS (1728–1779)
Queen Maria Amalia of Saxony, 1761
Oil on canvas, 60⅜ x 43⅜ in. (154 x 110 cm)

ENGLISH PAINTING

THOMAS LAWRENCE (1769–1830)
Miss Martha Carr, n.d.
Oil on canvas, 30 x 25¼ in. (76 x 64 cm)

DECORATIVE ARTS

The Dauphin's Treasure is incontestably among the Prado's most remarkable possessions, comprising objects of spectacular beauty. The Grand Dauphin, son of the French king Louis XIV and father of the Spanish king Philip V, had brought together in his chateau at Meudon, France, an enormous collection of objets d'art. At his death, in 1712, they were divided among his heirs; Philip V installed his portion at his summer palace in La Granja, Spain.

The Treasure consists primarily of Italian pieces from the sixteenth and seventeenth centuries, notably vases made of rock crystal and semiprecious stones (agate, jasper, lapis lazuli, turquoise, and so on) with gold and silver fittings. Because of its great value, the French looted the collection between 1813 and 1815, then subjected it to abuse. After its installation in the Prado in 1839, the Treasure was plundered once again in 1918, and during the Spanish Civil War it was sent to Geneva for safekeeping. Today, it is restored and installed in a manner befitting its magnificence.

In addition to the Treasure, the collection of decorative arts at the Prado also includes tapestries, pieces of Sèvres porcelain, and a fine group of Spanish items, from Talavera pottery to glassware from the La Granja workshops. There is also an important set of marble tables with the insets in precious gems that are known as *pietre dure*—some of Italian origin and others that were executed during the eighteenth century at the Buen Retiro workshops.

Onyx Salt Cellar with Gold Siren,
1st half of 16th century
Height: 6⅞ in. (17.5 cm)

Small Bark with Cupid Riding a Dragon, c. 1600
Agate, height: 12¼ in. (31 cm)

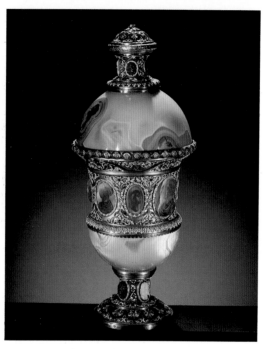

Oriental Vase with Cameos, 18th century
Chalcedony, height: 16⅛ in. (41 cm)

Basin of the Twelve Caesars, c. 1580
Vermeil, height: 16⅛ in. (41 cm)

Bark on Wheels, late 16th century
Rock crystal, 7⅞ x 15¾ in. (22 x 40 cm)

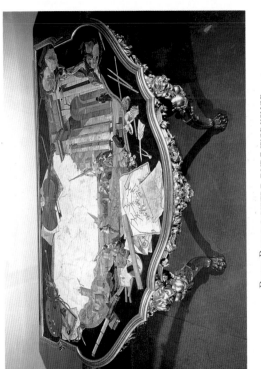

BUEN RETIRO PIETRE-DURE WORKSHOP
Console, 1770–80
Marble, agate, chalcedony, onyx, jasper, lapis lazuli, and
gilt bronze, 37⅞ x 69⅞ x 37 in. (96 x 177 x 94 cm)

FLORENTINE PIETRE-DURE WORKSHOP
Tabletop, 1616. Polychrome marble and *pietre dure*,
46⅜ x 46⅜ in. (118 x 118 cm)

ROMAN
Porphyry Table Supported by Lions, mid-17th century
Gilt bronze

SCULPTURE

The bulk of the Prado's sculpture collection, which includes some five hundred pieces, originated with the royal holdings. The incorporation of the Trinity Museum brought in several typically Spanish religious works; acquisitions made from the National Fine Arts Exhibitions and for a proposed museum of modern art explain the presence of a few works from the nineteenth century.

The holdings in classical sculpture, for the most part Greco-Roman and only recently catalogued, include various key items acquired over two centuries, from the reign of Philip II (*Venus with a Shell,* found at Sagonte) to the arrival, in 1724, of Prince Livio Odescalchi's collection, which had previously belonged to Queen Christina of Sweden. Another group of considerable importance comprises items that were unearthed at Tivoli, where excavations were overseen by Nicolás de Azara, the Spanish ambassador to Rome in 1779; the works he discovered were given to Charles IV. Among the most celebrated of these is the *San Ildefonso Group,* inspired by Polyclitus, and a *Bust of Antinoüs,* influenced by Praxiteles.

Another aspect of the sculpture collection, also directly linked to the history of Spain, includes works by Leone Leoni and his son Pompeo, Milanese sculptors in the service of Charles V and Philip II; *Emperor Charles V Mastering Fury,* a bronze statue, is among the major works of Italian sixteenth-century sculpture. There are also several Renaissance copies in bronze after antique models, which Velázquez brought back from Italy to decorate the Alcázar.

HELLENISTIC
San Ildefonso Group, 1st century B.C.
Marble, height: 63⅜ in. (161 cm)

ROMAN, INSPIRED BY A GREEK BRONZE OF 3D CENTURY B.C.
Faun with Kid, 2d century A.D.
Marble, height: 53½ in. (136 cm)

ROMAN
Venus with a Dolphin, 1st century A.D.
Marble, height: 78¾ in. (200 cm)

ROMAN
Bust of Antinoüs, imperial era
Marble, height: 38¼ in. (97 cm)

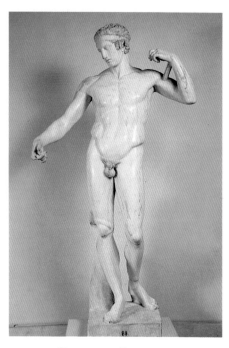

COPY AFTER POLYCLITUS
Diadumenes, n.d.
Marble, height: 79½ in. (202 cm)

GREEK FOLLOWER OF LYSIPPUS
Head, early 3d century A.D.
Bronze, height: 17⅝ in. (45 cm)

COPY OF AN ANCIENT ORIGINAL
Hermaphrodite, n.d.
Bronze, height: 61 in. (155 cm)

LEONE LEONI (1509–1590)
Emperor Charles V Mastering Fury, 1551–55
Bronze, 98¾ x 56⅜ in. (251 x 143 cm)

GIOVANNI BATTISTA FOGGINI (1652–1725)
Charles II, c. 1690
Gilt bronze, 38¼ x 17⅜ in. (97 x 44 cm)

INDEX OF ILLUSTRATIONS

309

Editors: Alice Gray and Nancy Grubb
Designer: Patrick Seymour
Production Editor: Abigail Asher
Production Manager: Matthew Pimm

First edition

   Library of Congress Cataloging-in-Publication Data
Garín Llombart, Felipe Vicente.
   Treasures of the Prado / Felipe Vicente Garín Llombart.
      p.   cm.
   Includes index.
   ISBN 1-55859-558-9
   1. Art—Spain—Madrid—Catalogs.   2. Museo del Prado—Catalogs.
   I. Title.
   N3450.A686   1993   93-20827
   708.6´41—dc20   CIP